Hilarious GENEROSITY

From the Bible-teaching ministry of

Charles R. Swindoll

INSIGHT FOR LIVING

Chuck graduated in 1963 from Dallas Theological Seminary, where he now serves as the school's fourth president, helping to prepare a new generation of men and women for the ministry. Chuck has served in pastorates in three states: Massachusetts, Texas, and California, including almost twenty-three years at the First Evangelical Free Church in Fullerton, California. His sermon messages have been aired over radio since 1979 as the *Insight for Living* broadcast. A best-selling author, Chuck has written numerous books and booklets on many subjects.

Based on the outlines and transcripts of Chuck's sermons, the study guide text is co-authored by Gary Matlack, a graduate of Texas Tech University and Dallas Theological Seminary. He also wrote the Living Insights sections.

Editor in Chief:
Cynthia Swindoll

Coauthor of Text:
Gary Matlack

Assistant Editor and Writer:
Wendy Peterson

Copy Editor:
Tom Kimber

Text Designer:
Gary Lett

Graphics System Administrator:
Bob Haskins

Publishing System Specialist:
Alex Pasieka

Director, Communications Division:
John Norton

Marketing Manager:
Alene Cooper

Project Coordinator:
Colette Muse

Printer:
Sinclair Printing Company

ISBN 0-8499-9952-9

Printed in the United States of America

COVER PHOTOGRAPH: Robert Nease

CONTENTS

INTRODUCTION

I t's my truck!"

"But you weren't playing with it; you were outside. Can't I play with it?"

"No! It's my truck!"

Getting a child to share a treasured toy is no easy task. He's even protective of it when he's not playing with it. He fears that once little sister curls her fingers around the toy, it's as good as gone. Mom's intervention and coercion may convince him to let it go, but he still won't be happy about it.

That's how many Christians are when it comes to giving. "It's my money! It's my time! It's my life!" And when we do share these with others, we often do so grudgingly, without joy.

There's a better way to live and give . . . God's way. I call it hilarious generosity. It starts in the heart, with a deep appreciation for all that God has given us—eternal treasures as well as material provisions for today. That appreciation, then, flows into our family, our church, our community, and our world through our generous and joyful giving.

Our time, talent and treasures are not toys to be grasped; they are gifts to be shared. In fact, God delights in our sharing them; He loves a cheerful giver (2 Cor. 9:7).

So let's explore some key biblical passages on giving and learn why it is truly more blessed to give than to receive.

Chuck Swindoll

Chuck Swindoll

PUTTING TRUTH INTO ACTION

K nowledge apart from application falls short of God's desire for His children. He wants us to apply what we learn so that we will change and grow. This study guide was prepared with these goals in mind. As you go through the following pages, we hope your desire to discover biblical truth will grow as your understanding of God's Word increases and that you will be encouraged to apply what you've learned.

To assist you in your study, we've included a section called Living Insights at the end of each lesson. These exercises will challenge you to study further and to think of specific ways to put your discoveries into action.

There are many ways to use this guide—in personal devotions, group studies, discussions with friends and family, and Sunday school classes. And, of course, it's an ideal study aid when you're listening to its corresponding *Insight for Living* radio series.

To benefit most from this study guide, we would encourage you to consider it a spiritual journal. That's why we've included space in the Living Insights for recording your thoughts and discoveries. We hope you'll return to those sections often for review and encouragement as you continue to grow in your walk with Christ.

Gary Matlack

Gary Matlack
Coauthor of Text
Author of Living Insights

Hilarious GENEROSITY

Chapter 1

A CASE FOR JOYFUL GENEROSITY

Selected Scriptures

There are two ways to give gifts. Chances are you've tried them both.

The first method goes something like this. You receive a wedding invitation from a fellow employee with whom you have no dealing outside of work. And you like it that way, since you get an ample dose of him at the office. Any social involvement would be bad medicine. Simply put, you just don't like the guy.

Suddenly, however, you're obligated to commit a chunk of your discretionary income to purchase a wedding gift for him and the woman you wish you knew well enough to ask, "What were you thinking?" Not only that, the wedding's in December, right around Christmas. That's when your budget, if it could make noise, would resemble that empty sucking sound at the bottom of a McDonald's milk shake. Not only do you have to shell out a small fortune for Christmas gifts, you have two birthdays coming up, a baby shower, the church Christmas party, and your neighbors' "we just bought a parakeet" gala. Even bird toys cost money!

At this point, it's probably safe to say that giving would rank down there with Novocain-free dental surgery on your list of desired activities. So about an hour before the wedding, you swing by J. C. Penney, snatch a cheap toaster from the housewares department, and ask them to gift wrap it for you—FAST! Not the most thoughtful gift, perhaps, but at least you got him something.

Contrast that scenario with this one. Your spouse is planning to retire this year. Besides the usual company farewell party, he's not expecting anything special to mark the occasion. But because you know how many people have enjoyed working with him and

1

have learned a great deal from him, you decide to throw him a surprise appreciation party. You want to acknowledge that his life's work has meant much more than just picking up a paycheck.

You start planning months ahead of time, contacting family members, friends, neighbors, past and present coworkers. They send you letters of appreciation, funny stories, even video clips for you to compile and present on that special night. You commission two of his musically inclined coworkers to compose a retirement song, which the whole group will sing at the event to salute his years of service. And the affair will be catered by his favorite restaurant.

Now, how would you feel about giving *that* gift? You would hardly be able to wait for the night to arrive.

What does the second scenario have that the first one doesn't? In a word, *joy*. There's a big difference between giving because you have to and giving because you want to. You might be surprised to discover that, though many Christians give grudgingly out of rote obligation, God wants His people to give joyfully from the heart.

A Key Passage on Giving

We find God's attitude about giving concisely expressed in Paul's second letter to the Corinthians.

> Let each one do just as he has purposed in his heart;
> not grudgingly or under compulsion; for God loves
> a cheerful giver. (2 Cor. 9:7)

The Context

A little background will help us appreciate the force of Paul's words. Corinth, you might remember, was an affluent city in first-century Greece. The church there, a year earlier, had pledged some funds to help the struggling church in Jerusalem. So Paul wrote to remind the Corinthians of their promise and to have them pull together the funds (2 Cor. 8:6–11), which he would collect on his next visit (9:4).

To help them do this, he would send Titus and others to Corinth to help the church get their financial house in order (8:6, 17–19, 22–24; 9:3). Paul would visit later with some of the Macedonians, to whom he had bragged about the Corinthians' willingness to give (9:2). And with the money already collected by then, there would be no embarrassment over the Corinthians' failure to follow through with their promise (v. 4).

Now, don't get the wrong idea. Paul wasn't twisting any arms. The Corinthians didn't need convincing that giving was a good thing; they just needed a little prodding to follow up on their previous pledge. They needed a bit of administration to go with their enthusiasm.

Also, avoiding embarrassment wasn't the only reason for the Corinthians to keep their promise. Besides the obvious benefit to the Jerusalem church, the Corinthians' joyful generosity would also benefit themselves in several ways.

Sowing and Reaping

First of all, they would enjoy a return on their "investment."

> Now this I say, he who sows sparingly shall also
> reap sparingly; and he who sows bountifully shall
> also reap bountifully. (2 Cor. 9:6)

Paul applies a well-known agricultural proverb to the Corinthians' finances. If a farmer sows sparingly, he can expect a skimpy harvest. But if he scatters his seed generously, he can anticipate a bountiful crop.

Is this a blanket guarantee that if we give generously to the needy we will suddenly find ourselves rolling in dough? Not at all. If we look ahead to verse 10, we find Paul pointing to "the harvest of your righteousness"—clearly referring to much more than a material harvest. In other words, the more we give to God's work, the more God provides for us so we can keep on giving (v. 11a). Our generosity, in turn, sows seeds of thankfulness to God in others (vv. 11b–12), directing hearts toward Him and thereby glorifying Him at the same time (v. 13; see also Matt. 5:16). A life that points back to God's grace is certainly a rich harvest, as is the prayer support of other believers who are encouraged by our example (2 Cor. 9:14).

Giving Cheerfully

Besides sowing bountifully, the Corinthians are called to give cheerfully, for God delights in the generosity of His children.

> Let each one do just as he has purposed in his heart;
> not grudgingly or under compulsion; for God loves
> a cheerful giver. (v. 7)

Notice that the Lord specifically delights in a "cheerful" giver. What's a cheerful giver? Someone who gives from the heart, whose giving flows from the inside out. This desire isn't manufactured by coercion or guilt. It isn't forced on someone. The words *grudgingly* and *under compulsion* suggest someone who would rather hold on to his or her possessions but feels pressured to turn them loose.

Conversely, a "cheerful" giver considers the opportunity, makes his or her own decision, and gives accordingly. *Hilaros*, the Greek word for *cheerful*, does not appear anywhere else in Scripture. How interesting that of all the places it could appear, it turns up here in a passage about giving. Perhaps that's because God knew we needed some joy in that area of life. Maybe He wants to see us smile more often when we drop the check in the offering plate. Maybe we need to see tithing and missions and feeding the hungry as more than obligations. Could it be that, by giving with such long faces (or not giving at all), we Christians are missing a wonderful opportunity to express our love to God . . . and sense His love for us?

We can certainly extend this principle beyond the financial realm to anything we give—time, talent, service, advice. These can be pulled from us like stubborn weeds, or we can let them blossom naturally from a joyful heart.

Cheerful Givers from the Bible

Still wondering what a cheerful giver looks like? If so, you need look no further than the pages of Scripture.

The Ancient Israelites

Having freed the Hebrews from Egyptian bondage, God now wanted to dwell among His people. So He gave Moses instructions for building a tabernacle, where the presence of the Lord would dwell. But where would the building materials come from in the wilderness? From the people's possessions.

To God, this was more than just a building project. It was a statement about His holiness, His love for His people, and His desire for them to draw close to Him. For He wanted more than their jewels, linens, and gold—He wanted their hearts. So He told Moses,

> "Tell the sons of Israel to raise a contribution for Me; from every man whose heart moves him you shall raise My contribution." (Exod. 25:2; see also 35:5–9)

How did they respond?

> Then all the congregation of the sons of Israel departed from Moses' presence. And everyone whose

heart stirred him and everyone whose spirit moved him came and brought the Lord's contribution for the work of the tent of meeting and for all its service and for the holy garments. . . . The Israelites, all the men and women, whose heart moved them to bring material for all the work, which the Lord had commanded through Moses to be done, brought a freewill offering to the Lord. (35:20–21, 29; see also vv. 22–28)

That's cheerful giving! You can almost see the Israelites picking through their jewelry and shaking out their fine linen. You can hear the jingling and clanking of the trinkets as they're handed to Moses. You can almost smell the fragrance of spice rising from the camp as jars of it were collected for worship. All this activity represented giving that grew out of a love for God and a longing for His presence.

They gave so much, in fact, that Moses had to tell them to stop (Exod. 36:5–7). They had collected more than enough to build the tabernacle.

Nehemiah

Nehemiah served as cupbearer to King Artaxerxes of Persia. Upon hearing that the wall around his homeland, Jerusalem, lay in ruins, Nehemiah's soul was stirred to return there and rebuild the wall. Jerusalem, after all, was God's city, the place where His temple had stood and had just been rebuilt after the Babylonian captivity. Nehemiah couldn't let the city lay unprotected and become a disgrace before the nations.

So he obtained the king's permission to return there—and Artaxerxes even provided the raw materials needed for the project (Neh. 2:8)! Nehemiah then motivated the people to rebuild the wall, and they completed it only fifty-two days (6:15). Did he twist their arms? No. Did he use guilt to motivate them? No. They participated because of their desire to see Jerusalem rise again and God's named honored among the nations. They "worked with all their heart" (4:6 NIV). If only more of our religious activity would flow from that kind of cheerful, giving spirit, who knows what the church could accomplish in our day?

The Magi

Gold, frankincense, and myrrh. These were precious gifts of joy given by men who traveled from a foreign country to worship the

Christ child (Matt. 2:11). No one told the wise men, "Hey, you guys better make an appearance at that birthday party in Bethlehem." They didn't go reluctantly. No, they couldn't wait to find the Child and lavish their gifts upon Him. When the star pinpointed Jesus' location, "They rejoiced exceedingly with great joy" (v. 10).

Jesus Christ

We saved the best example for last. No one has given as much as our Lord gave for us. He stepped out of heaven to live among us. He lived a perfect life, though tempted, ridiculed, and persecuted. And He allowed Himself to be dragged through a farcical trial, beaten, and hung on a cross. There He suffered the wrath of His own Father so we wouldn't have to and so we could become righteous in God's sight.

He gave it all. Yet He gave it with joy, as the book of Hebrews tells us:

> . . . fixing our eyes on Jesus, the author and perfecter of faith, who for the joy set before Him endured the cross, despising the shame, and has sat down at the right hand of the throne of God. (Heb. 12:2)

Christ's gift of salvation tells us that joyful giving involves more than a smile on the face and a skip in the step. Real joy is deeper than that. It involves the pleasure of doing God's will, and it delights in the success of another. Real joy can accompany any circumstance, no matter how difficult.

Though our redemption came at such a painful price, God was pleased to arrange it. And Christ accomplished it with joy.

How can we, who have received so much from Christ, be anything but cheerful givers?

> For you know the grace of our Lord Jesus Christ, that though He was rich, yet for your sake He became poor, that you through His poverty might become rich.
> . . . Thanks be to God for His indescribable gift! (2 Cor. 8:9; 9:15)

6

1 Tim 6: 17, 18 - Be not highminded, nor trust in uncertainity of riches, but in the living God who gives us richly all things to enjoy. (18) That they do good, that they be rich in good works, ready to distribute, willing to communicate

Living Insights

Has your giving been drained of joy for some reason? If so, here are some hints for restoring it.

1. *Reflect on God's gifts to you.* Joyful receivers make joyful givers. By reflecting on all that God has given us, we can keep the joy level high in our own giving. What do you have to be thankful for? Start with your salvation in Christ, then let your mind roam over all the many big and little things. If you want some help getting started, consider all that the psalmist was thankful for in Psalm 103.

Mercy
Grace
Guidance
Peace
Help w/ finances
Strength
Patience

2. *Remind yourself of His promises.* God has promised to bless not only the recipient of the gift but the giver as well. Look up the following verses, and jot down one or two that especially speak to your heart.

Ecclesiastes 11:1   Luke 14:12–14
Matthew 6:3–4   2 Corinthians 9:6–7
Luke 6:38   1 Timothy 6:18–19

Matt 6:3 Luke 6:38 Give & it shall be given to you. Same as you give it will be returned

Luke 14:12-14 - When you make a feast, don't call friends, they try to pay you back but call the lame, the poor, the maimed the blind, they cannot pay you. And you shall be blessed.

3. *Examine your heart.* "How does God want *me* to give?" That's the question we all need to ask. Don't compare your giving habits with those of the Joneses. Don't use your pastor's convictions as the sole criteria, either. Examine your own heart. Ask yourself some questions like:

- "What need do I feel drawn to?"

So many needs of my own, I cannot open up to feel the need of someone else. Maybe only Andre maybe Pete Cathy & Chris

- "Am I giving because I feel pressured or because I really want to give?"

I want to

- "What resources has God blessed me with that would help build up the body of Christ?"

Knowledge in certain areas, everything else is depleted, money terms

- "Am I giving at an appropriate level for my income?"

Nothing to give - Am I to give anyway & let something go unpaid

- "What do I have a real passion for?"

4. *Be generous.* We need to give wisely and responsibly. But there is also a sense in which we should give beyond our means, <u>give extravagantly now and then and watch</u> God bless our generosity. Consider the early church in Jerusalem who "had all things in

common" (Acts 2:44). They sold property and possessions and gave the proceeds to those in need. And God blessed the church with growth, fellowship, and a sweet sense of community.

Has God been leading your heart toward a particularly extravagant act of generosity? How have you discerned this? How has it been different from giving impetuously?

Too overburdened, can't see ways of giving. God, Father, Open my heart & mind to see your will for my giving during this stage of my life.

What is it that you feel He is leading you to do?

?

How can you make generosity—in both small and extravagant things—your way of life?

Be consistent

Chapter 2

ENJOYING THE BENEFITS
OF GENEROSITY

1 Timothy 6:6–10, 17–19

"If I only had more, I could give more."

That's the thinking many of us fall into when we consider our own giving habits. When we think like this, though, we miss the point. Joyful giving doesn't depend on our *accumulation* of money as much as it does on our *attitude* toward it. The sum of what we give isn't nearly as important as the spirit in which we give it. We don't have to be wealthy to give joyfully, but we do have to be healthy in how we view our possessions, whether few or many.

Joyful giving, in other words, begins with contentment. The less we depend on material things to make us happy, the more likely we are to give more of them away.

If contentment must be present for joyful giving to occur, then we need to know what contentment is . . . and what it is not. So let's take some time to define contentment and see how to hold onto it in a world that tries so hard to take it away.

Contentment Analyzed

Some define *contentment* as a whimsical, "not-a-care-in-the-world" state of mind. It's a place to which we all want to escape. Where pleasure and play rule the day—like the Hundred Acre Wood, where Winnie the Pooh, after polishing off a whole jar of honey, plops himself against a tree for a sticky, satisfying nap (without losing his job).

Others see contentment as something to be avoided. It's a dangerous spiritual enemy, they say. Contentment means being satisfied with mediocrity, settling for what makes us happy instead of what makes us holy.

The scriptural definition avoids these two extremes. God's Word

---

This chapter has been adapted from "Contentment . . . and How to Miss It," in the study guide *Excellence in Ministry: A Study of 1 Timothy*, coauthored by Gary Matlack, from the Bible-teaching ministry of Charles R. Swindoll (Anaheim, Calif.: Insight for Living, 1996).

portrays contentment as a desirable trait, a level of satisfaction every Christian should experience. Yet contentment functions in the realm of reality; it retains responsibility and righteousness. Properly understood, contentment graces the Christian life and fosters both gratitude and generosity.

The Meaning of Contentment

Let's start with what contentment is *not*. It's not laziness or selfishness. And it's certainly not complacency. Scripture denounces all of these qualities (see Prov. 6:6–11; 1 Cor. 10:24; Phil. 3:8–14). Nor is it satisfaction with mediocrity. Our God, after all, is an excellent God. And whatever we do, including giving, should reflect His excellence.

The Greek root of *content*, *arkeō*, suggests the idea of sufficiency, that something is enough. When what we have—including our financial status, material possessions, and physical appearance—is enough, then we are free from turmoil over our lot. We are at peace rather than worried, afraid, panicky, or ruthlessly competitive and greedy.

Paul's use of the term in 1 Timothy and other epistles, according to commentator Duane Litfin, expresses "that inner God-given sufficiency which does not depend on material circumstances."[1] John the Baptizer used the same root word when he urged his listeners to be content with their wages (Luke 3:14). Jesus implied the importance of contentment when he warned, "Be on your guard against every form of greed" (Luke 12:15). The writer of Hebrews also contrasted greed with contentment:

> Let your character be free from the love of money, being content with what you have; for He Himself has said, "I will never desert you, nor will I ever forsake you," so that we confidently say,
> "The Lord is my helper, I will not be afraid. What shall man do to me?" (Heb. 13:5–6)

---

1. A. Duane Litfin, "1 Timothy," in *The Bible Knowledge Commentary*, New Testament edition, ed. John F. Walvoord and Roy B. Zuck (Wheaton, Ill.: Scripture Press Publications, Victor Books, 1983), p. 746. See also 2 Corinthians 9:8 and Philippians 4:11 for other uses of the same word.

Contentment, then, has to do with recognizing the sufficiency of what we have—especially what we have in Christ (see Rom. 8:32; 1 Tim. 6:17). And that recognition carries with it many benefits.

The Benefits of Contentment

First, *contentment allows current enjoyment rather than constant striving.* Content Christians don't have to wait until their salary reaches six figures to be happy. Their quality of life doesn't depend on the "Someday I'lls": "Someday, I'll have a new house; then I'll be happy." "Someday, I'll be married (or single again); then I'll enjoy life." "Someday, I'll join the perfect church; then I'll start to grow." Because contentment flows from the heart, it allows us to enjoy the here and now. Real contentment doesn't feed on circumstances or wishful thinking.

Second, *contentment gives us freedom to recognize and applaud another's achievements without being eaten up with envy.* Contentment releases us from unhealthy competition and comparison. The more content we are with our own lives, the more we can celebrate another's success instead of falling prey to jealousy.

Third, *contentment enables us to develop a genuinely grateful spirit.* Those who lack contentment don't know what it means to be truly thankful. By focusing on what they don't have, they lose sight of all the blessings—spiritual and material—that God has provided. And thankless people make poor Christians. Gratitude is the cornerstone of an effective witness for Christ (see 1 Thess. 5:18; Heb. 13:15).

Contentment's Companion: Godliness

It's no surprise that the apostle Paul addressed the topic of contentment with Timothy, his protégé. With all that the young pastor had to face in Ephesus, contentment might have seemed elusive to him at times. False teachers assaulted Timothy's message. Some people discounted him because of his youth. And the needs of widows were outpacing the people's ability to meet them. Such circumstances could easily dampen anyone's desire to give and serve.

In Paul's first letter to Timothy, he presents the importance of contentment by showing how it intertwines with another crucial characteristic: godliness.

The Meaning of Godliness

In 1 Timothy 6:3–5, Paul describes false teachers who, among their other unsavory characteristics, consider a pious veneer a path to prosperity. There's money to be made in religion, they believe—fleecing the flock isn't too difficult if you can look and talk the part. Warning Timothy to avoid such thinking, Paul encourages his friend that true godliness has a very real reward of its own—especially if it's enhanced by contentment.

> But godliness actually is a means of great gain, when accompanied by contentment. (v. 6)

When we speak of godliness, we mean more than external piety. Being godly is to live one's life with Christ in clear focus, to have a prevailing desire to obey God, to take Him seriously regardless, to deliberately pursue holiness.

The Benefits of Godliness

What are some of the specific ways we profit from living a godly life? Here are just a few of the benefits.

1. *A godly mind-set increases our ability to differentiate between the temporal and the eternal.* With godliness at the forefront of our minds, we are better able to make discerning priorities and avoid the pitfalls of immediate gratification and fleeting pleasures.

2. *A godly heart increases our sensitivity toward God and other people.* Godliness nurtures within us a humble, listening spirit that picks up on the sometimes subtle proddings of the Lord and the often unstated needs and feelings of others around us.

3. *A godly character fosters a willingness to live within circumstantial limits.* Rather than sinking into the mire of self-doubt, pessimistic dissatisfaction, and bitter grumbling, godliness helps us rest in the Lord's care and encourages us with hope.

So, to return to Paul's affirmation in verse 6, godliness plus contentment equals great gain. And that gain goes beyond mere material wealth, which is destroyed by moth and rust and stolen by thieves (Matt. 6:19–21). It is the imperishable treasure of heaven, that inner peace and satisfaction of being right with God, of obeying and loving Him, of knowing that His generosity is richly bestowed on each of us (see Ps. 16:11; Eph. 1:3–8a; 2:7).

Contentment and Generosity

A godly contentment, then—a reverent and joyful spirit that celebrates all God has given us—is indeed a means of great gain. Not great loss or passive sacrifice or a spiritless settling for less, but gain. This means we can approach life with an abundance mentality instead of a scarcity mentality: with the confidence that God can and will supply more than enough for everyone, rather than fearing there's not enough to go around (see Rom. 8:32; 1 Cor. 3:21–23).

When we realize the vastness of our resources through God, that the eternal richness of heaven is His gift to us, we won't be miserly with the things we have but eager and free to share. In short, we will know the joy of generosity.

A generosity rooted in godly contentment also has some priceless benefits. Let's rejoin Paul in 1 Timothy 6 to see what they are.

We Hold Temporal Things Loosely

> For we have brought nothing into the world, so we cannot take anything out of it either. (v. 7)

Since we enter this world carrying nothing, wearing nothing, owning nothing, and we leave the same way, why should we cling to our earthly goods? Generosity rooted in contentment allows us to say with Job, "Naked I came from my mother's womb, And naked I shall return there" (Job 1:21a)—and know that all we have in between comes from God's kind hands.

We Keep Our Essentials to a Minimum

> And if we have food and covering, with these we shall be content. (1 Tim. 6:8)

We may enter and exit this world naked, but we all need certain possessions for survival during our sojourn here. We need food, water, clothing, and shelter, for example. These are essentials. Now, that doesn't mean it's wrong to own a car, a stereo, or jewelry. But we should never depend on them for our contentment.

The "he who dies with the most toys wins" attitude promotes an empty life because it never satisfies. It starts with the "need" to have a bigger, more expensive car. Then a boat. Then a summer home or two. Then . . . satisfaction eludes us. We have made luxuries into essentials.

A generosity rooted in contentment, however, helps us keep

~~focused on what's really necessary for ourselves—and what's needed for others.~~

We Withstand the Appealing Allure of Greed

Contrasted with those who are content with the basics are those who want to amass wealth.

> But those who want to get rich fall into temptation and a snare and many foolish and harmful desires which plunge men into ruin and destruction. For the love of money is a root of all sorts of evil, and some by longing for it have wandered away from the faith, and pierced themselves with many a pang. (vv. 9–10)

Those who are driven by the love of money have as their guiding light the glitter of silver and gold, which lures them to their destruction (see also Prov. 20:21; 28:20, 22). Philip H. Towner vividly describes the downward spiral taken by those whose life's passion is for riches.

> First, the pursuit of wealth leads down a road filled with every variety of pitfall. The words *temptation* and *trap* may well be used with Satan's manipulations in mind (3:7), and the Enemy is certainly capable of using the hope of wealth to blur the moral distinctions of believers. *Foolish and harmful desires* not only are for wealth itself but are probably also immoral cravings unleashed by access to wealth. Wealth leads people into circles where the rules are different, the peer pressure is tremendous, and the values are totally distorted. What, for the believer, might have been unthinkable from the outside becomes quite natural once on the inside. And the end of this is utter devastation, which Paul emphasizes with a verb that means to *plunge* (as if to drown) and two nouns that combine to describe complete *destruction*. Let the reader beware, for there are no such warning signs along the path to riches.[2]

2. Philip H. Towner, *1–2 Timothy and Titus*, The IVP New Testament Commentary Series (Downers Grove, Ill.: InterVarsity Press, 1994), p. 139.

The lure of money is even strong enough to entice some away from the faith, leaving the debris of broken promises and relationships in its wake (1 Tim. 6:10).

Notice, though, that money itself is not the problem; our attitude toward it is. Money is amoral, neither good nor bad. But the "love of money" is the root of all kinds of evil and leads to destruction. Put another way, it's not what we have that causes problems, it's what has us.

When we have a contented, generous spirit, however, God has us and our possessions, and greed has no place to take root.

We Cultivate a Lifestyle That Is Truly Joyful

What about those who are already rich? How are they to view their wealth?

> Instruct those who are rich in this present world not to be conceited or to fix their hope on the uncertainty of riches, but on God, who richly supplies us with all things to enjoy. (v. 17)

First, Paul says that the rich are to avoid being conceited, looking down on those who have less (see also Prov. 14:21; 17:5; 22:2). Second, they're not to fix their hope on a false security (see also Prov. 23:4–5). And third, we are all to see our possessions as belonging to God and given by Him for His glory and our enjoyment.

Yes, *our enjoyment.* God is not a pleasure-squasher but a pleasure-provider. He just doesn't want us to be deceived by the world's false joys that turn bitter the morning after. Rather, He wants us to realize that an absence of conceit plus the presence of security will equal true, lasting joy.

Enjoying the Benefits of Contented Generosity

Do you want to multiply your joys? Put some "hilarity" in your spirit? Then take to heart Paul's counsel in 1 Timothy 6.18–19.

First, "do good" (v. 18a). Use your money for worthwhile causes. Do good with it!

Second, "be rich in good works, . . . be generous" (v. 18b). Give yourself as fully and freely as you give your material goods.

Third, "be . . . ready to share" (v. 18c). The verse really suggests *staying* ready to share—being quick and thoughtful, sensitive and current.

16

Fourth, store up "the treasure of a good foundation for the future, so that you may take hold of that which is life indeed" (v. 19). Today's actions invest in eternity's future. Our goal, then, is not "the good life" but the *true life*, the real life that is hidden in Christ (see Col. 3:2–4).

Jesus said, "It is more blessed to give than to receive" (Acts 20:35). When we live with godly contentment, we can know the blessing of giving with joy.

 Living Insights

Would you define yourself as a contented person? *Somewhat*
If so, how does your contentment show? Do you enjoy giving? Do you often think about ways to meet the needs of others? Do you tend to keep cars, appliances, and other items around as long as they work, without feeling that you have to rush out and buy the latest model? Is yours a lifestyle of simplicity?

Not doing that which I can't afford. Yes I enjoy giving. Not ways but would like to meet others needs. Do keep things around don't have to have latest model. Somewhat

If you're not content, explore some possible reasons why you may be missing this quality. Do you compare your lifestyle to that of others, trying to "keep up with the Joneses"? Are you attaching too much importance to earthly treasures and not enough to heavenly ones? Do you feel that you have to accumulate more than you have now to be truly happy? Are you waiting to "have it all" before you start enjoying life or giving to others? Do you always have to rush out and buy the newest and best of everything in order to feel fulfilled? What do you spend your time praying for?

Feel I have to accumulate more to be right - to pay who I owe. Not desiring to live lavish but to pay bills. I spend my time praying for others, & guidance

17

See any attitudes or actions that need to change? How about bringing those before the Lord now.

Lord, I'm not sure. Maybe I'm not content as I should be. Just want to break even & to pay those I owe. Where did I do wrong — Not contented on Kester. But we were bulging at the seam — too many.

Chapter 3

VALUABLE PRINCIPLES OF
MONEY MANAGEMENT
Selected Proverbs

Just give it to me in plain English; I'm not a computer expert."
How many of us have used such words when trying to understand something about which we know very little? We don't want the auto mechanic to give us a technical lecture about our car's electrical system; we just want to know why the thing won't start. And we don't usually want to get tangled up in the intricacies of the free market system; we just want to know where to invest our retirement savings. When we go to the doctor, we don't want the Latin name of the virus that has taken up residence in our body; we just want our throat to stop hurting.

Simplicity. That's what most of us want when it comes to learning, isn't it? Good, helpful information, user-friendly, wrapped in layman's terms.

A company called IDG Books Worldwide has tapped into the need for simplicity. You may have seen some of their "For Dummies" books at your local bookstore. They have *PCs for Dummies*, *College Planning for Dummies*, *Everyday Math for Dummies*, *Personal Finance for Dummies*, *VCRs and Camcorders for Dummies*, *Politics for Dummies*, *Parenting for Dummies*, and yes, even *Sex for Dummies*.

The books are selling like crazy! According to IDG's home page on the World Wide Web, the publisher currently has nearly four hundred titles in print and foreign translations in thirty languages. Their method is simple: Find an expert in a certain field, and have him or her write to educate nonexperts about that topic. Now readers all over the world are learning about subjects they were once too intimidated to pursue. Instead of technical jargon, readers get easy-to-understand terms, humor, a conversational style, memory-aiding visuals, and practicality.

IDG Books, however, isn't the only place to look for lessons made simple. Just take a look at the Proverbs. Concise, pithy, uncomplicated, bite-sized nuggets of wisdom. But, oh so profound. We could subtitle Proverbs, "The Spiritual Life for Dummies."

And since many Proverbs address the topic of material wealth, what better source is there to consult about how to manage our money wisely?

A Few Clarifications regarding Proverbs

Before turning to the verses that specifically address money, it will be helpful to consider a few facts about Proverbs in general.

First, *Proverbs is an ancient book, but its contents are timeless and relevant.* God's wisdom for living, like God himself, never changes. Proverbs speaks to twentieth-century saints tempted by lust, greed, laziness, anger, and pride just as poignantly as it spoke to people who struggled with those same issues in Solomon's day.

Second, *the book as a whole is difficult to outline, but most of the individual verses are easy to understand.* Proverbs is not a narrative book—it's not a developing story like Genesis or Acts. Rather, it's a collection of clear maxims that address practical living. So it's not the easiest book in the Bible to chart or outline. But that's OK. The book was meant to be chewed and digested in small bites, one rich and savory verse at a time. Overanalysis and overorganization could very well spoil the meal.[1]

Third, *the topics are numerous and varied, but each subject can be developed in a unified way.* For example, you'll find the topic of money scattered throughout Proverbs; there's no single section that deals with money, or with pride, etc. The best way to study a topic in Proverbs is to look up that subject and related key words in a concordance, which is an alphabetical listing of words in Scripture. Then spend some time exploring each of the Scripture references listed for those words.

This particular message came out of Chuck's concordance study of the financially related terms in Proverbs: *money, gold, silver, lending, borrowing, riches,* etc.

Fourth, *it's important that we understand the difference between Proverbs and promises.* Commentator Sid S. Buzzell reminds us that

As brief maxims, the verses in Proverbs are distilled, to-the-point sentences about life. They boil

---

1. Though we can't tightly outline Proverbs, we can note the three types of proverbs in the book. First are *contrastive*, as in Proverbs 13:1: "A wise son accepts his father's discipline, But a scoffer does not listen to rebuke." Next are *completive*, as in 16:3: "Commit your works to the Lord, And your plans will be established." And last are *comparative*, as in 15:16: "Better is a little with the fear of the Lord, Than great treasure and turmoil with it."

down, crystallize, and condense the experiences and observations of the writers. . . . They tell what life is like and how life should be lived. . . .

Many of the proverbial maxims should be recognized as guidelines, not absolute observations; they are not iron-clad promises.[2]

This doesn't make the Proverbs less inspired or less true than the rest of Scripture, nor does it show any flaw or inconsistency in God's nature. It's simply a recognition of the literary form and purpose of Proverbs.

Some Timeless Principles of Money Management

Emerging from the many verses in Proverbs that deal with the topic of money are six key principles.

Principle 1: Those Who Honor God with Their Wealth Are Blessed in Return

Remember our earlier discussion of 2 Corinthians 9:7, which says, "God loves a cheerful giver"? Indeed He does. And He demonstrates His love for cheerful giving by blessing those who give.

Honor the Lord from your wealth,
And from the first of all your produce;
So your barns will be filled with plenty,
And your vats will overflow with new wine.
(Prov. 3:9–10)

Verse 9 is a command; verse 10, the result of obeying that command. Notice what priority giving to the Lord should be—first (v. 9b). To those in an Old Testament agrarian society, that meant giving the first crops of the new harvest to the Lord.

We honor God by first giving to Him from our paycheck. In doing so, we acknowledge His ownership of everything before we enjoy any of it ourselves. Whatever your income, give a portion to the Lord first. He will be honored and glorified by your trust. And He will bless you (see also Luke 6:38).

---

2. Sid S. Buzzell, "Proverbs," in *The Bible Knowledge Commentary*, Old Testament edition, ed. John F. Walvoord and Roy B. Zuck (Wheaton, Ill.: Scripture Press Publications, Victor Books, 1985), p. 904.

Principle 2: Those Who Make Riches Their Passion Lose More Than They Gain

"Make as much as you can as fast as you can." That philosophy, which pervades American society, may seem like the path to abundance. But just the opposite is true.

> Do not weary yourself to gain wealth,
> Cease from your consideration of it.
> When you set your eyes on it, it is gone.
> For wealth certainly makes itself wings,
> Like an eagle that flies toward the heavens.
> (Prov. 23:4–5)

There's nothing wrong with having wealth, in and of itself. And we should all pursue excellence and competence in our field, whatever our profession. This, in turn, often leads to financial success. But when having more, more, more becomes life's all-consuming desire, the most important treasures in life—God, family, friendships, personal health, constructive leisure—fall by the wayside (see also 10:22; 13:21; 15:27; 28:20–22).

Principle 3: Wisdom Gives Wealth Needed Guidance

Want a picture of wealth without wisdom? How about the lottery winner who squanders all his winnings at the racetrack trying to win even more money. Wealth needs wisdom to guide it. Otherwise, money is just another tool for foolishness. And if you have to choose between wealth and wisdom, choose wisdom.

> "Take my instruction, and not silver,
> And knowledge rather than choicest gold.
> For wisdom is better than jewels;
> And all desirable things can not compare with
> her."
> (Prov. 8:10–11; see also vv. 18–21; 16:16)

We should seek wisdom first. Then, whether wealth comes or not, we have what we need to live a life rich toward God (see Luke 12:16–21).

Principle 4: Increased Riches Bring Increased Complications

This principle also dispels some rumors. Many people think that if they had unlimited wealth, they could do whatever they want, whenever they want, without distraction or a care in the world. Not so! Just look at some of the problems that can accompany wealth.

A *false sense of security:*

> A rich man's wealth is his strong city,
> And like a high wall in his own imagination.
> (Prov. 18:11)

Excessive wealth can make us feel smug, secure, untouchable, unaccountable . . . and able to make it without the Lord. So beware! These fleeting feelings will one day dissipate like fog and reveal reality—the rich and the poor answer to the same God (22:2).

Many new "friends":

> The poor is hated even by his neighbor,
> But those who love the rich are many. . . .
> Wealth adds many friends,
> But a poor man is separated from his friend.
> (14:20; 19:4)

Money draws people like a picnic draws ants. When people find out you have money, they tend to swarm around, waiting to carry off a slice of the pie.

Pride and arrogance:

> The poor man utters supplications,
> But the rich man answers roughly.
> (18:23; see also 28:11)

Wealth often brings with it an "I'm better than you" attitude. Many of those who have acquired significant wealth have forgotten how to treat people. They look down their noses at those who have less. Another proverb speaks to this kind of attitude:

> Pride goes before destruction,
> And a haughty spirit before stumbling.
> (16:18)

Principle 5: Money Cannot Buy Life's Most Valuable Possessions

The Beatles had it right—money *can't* buy love:

> Better is a dish of vegetables where love is,
> Than a fattened ox and hatred with it.
> (Prov. 15:17)

Money can't buy a lot of the things that really matter. Like integrity (28:6), peace (15:16), or a good reputation (22:1). Full pockets don't guarantee godly character. The most valuable things in life are not for sale. Money will buy:

A bed BUT NOT sleep.
Books BUT NOT brains.
Food BUT NOT appetite.
Finery BUT NOT beauty.
A house BUT NOT a home.
Medicine BUT NOT health.
Luxuries BUT NOT culture.
Amusement BUT NOT happiness.
A crucifix BUT NOT a Saviour.
A church-pew BUT NOT heaven.[3]

Principle 6: If Handled Wisely, Money Can Bring Encouragement; If Mishandled, Great Stress

A good man leaves an inheritance to his children's children,
And the wealth of the sinner is stored up for the righteous. (13:22)

Those who handle their money wisely will have some left over to help others, including members of their own family. Conversely, those who misuse it will have little to share.

The rich rules over the poor,
And the borrower becomes the lender's slave. . . .
Do not be among those who give pledges,
Among those who become sureties for debts.
If you have nothing with which to pay,
Why should he take your bed from under you?
(Prov. 22:7, 26–27)

Excessive debt shackles funds that could be used to help people in need. Don't immerse yourself in debt just so you can accumulate more possessions. As much as possible, stay out of debt . . . so you can give with hilarity.

---

3. *Encyclopedia of 7,700 Illustrations: Signs of the Times,* comp. Paul Lee Tan (Chicago, Ill.: Assurance Publishers, 1979), p. 832.

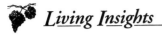 *Living Insights*

Perhaps this is the first time you've come to grips with money, and particularly giving, as a spiritual endeavor. Interesting, isn't it? We have no trouble viewing worship, evangelism, even fellowship, as spiritual activities. But managing our finances? That sounds so, well, "nonsupernatural." So mundane, so mechanical.

But the Bible tells us that how we handle our money is a barometer for gauging our spiritual health. Jesus knew the rich young ruler would never embrace Him, because he couldn't turn loose of his earthly possessions (see Luke 18:18–25). Peter detected the spiritual condition of Simon the Sorcerer right away, because the man saw money, not the Spirit, as the way to spiritual power (Acts 8:18–24). And Paul? We've already seen how he felt about money: True believers who name the name of Christ should give to help spread the gospel and build the church (2 Cor. 9).

If someone were to flip through your checkbook, examine your sales receipts, and analyze your family budget, what would they say about your spiritual life?

It's Pretty good

Maybe the best way to manage our money is to first let God manage our hearts. For example, a nagging lack of contentment or trust in God can prompt us to spend more money on material possessions than we should. An unhealthy detachment from Christ's church can keep us from giving toward the spread of the gospel. And bitterness over past hurts can make us resistant to being as generous as we might be. Is there anything you need to take care of spiritually that will show up in how you manage your finances?

Do I need to give to you first — to the top — to fix things

No matter how you add it up, our first order of business is to walk with the Savior.

Chapter 4

A Joyful Plan That Cannot Fail

Selected Scriptures

Now that you have seen what the Bible has to say about joyful giving, there's only one thing left to do—become a joyful giver. That is, if you're not one already.

If you're not, it could be that you don't have a plan for regular, systematic giving. Well, you're in luck. The purpose of this chapter is to help you develop such a plan. Because a joyful giver is a deliberate and consistent giver.

A Required Plan: The Ancient Hebrews

In preparing to formulate a personal plan for giving, let's examine the practices of those who lived in biblical times. Was there a prescribed pattern of giving in those days? We can answer that question by first looking at the lives of the ancient Israelites.

Tithing before the Law

Tithing (returning one-tenth of one's income to God) was the normal practice of giving in the Old Testament. It was prescribed in the Mosaic Law (see Lev. 27:30–33; Num. 18:26), but it started long before God chiseled His commandments into stone at Sinai. We find tithing practiced as early as Abraham's day.

> Then after [Abram's] return from the defeat of Chedorlaomer and the kings who were with him, the king of Sodom went out to meet him at the valley of Shaveh (that is, the King's Valley). And Melchizedek king of Salem brought out bread and wine; now he was a priest of God Most High. And he blessed him and said,
>
> > "Blessed be Abram of God Most High,
> > Possessor of heaven and earth;
> > And blessed be God Most High,
> > Who has delivered your enemies into your hand."

And [Abram] gave him a tenth of all. (Gen. 14:17–20; see also Heb. 7:1–2)

Abraham had just defeated King Chedorlaomer and all the forces that sacked Sodom and Gomorrah and captured Abraham's nephew, Lot. A king-priest named Melchizedek came out to bless Abraham and publicly acknowledge God's protection and power. In response, Abraham "gave him a tenth of all," an act that recognized Melchizedek as a priest of the true God.

Abraham's grandson Jacob also offered tithes to the Lord. The morning after God revealed Himself in a dream to Jacob at Bethel, the patriarch set up a sacred stone to commemorate the event. Then he made a vow, saying,

> "If God will be with me and will keep me on this journey that I take, and will give me food to eat and garments to wear, and I return to my father's house in safety, then the Lord will be my God. And this stone, which I have set up as a pillar, will be God's house; and of all that Thou dost give me I will surely give a tenth to Thee." (Gen. 28:20–22)

Long before tithing was a legal mandate, then, it was an act of devotion and worship from a heart that loved God.

Tithing under the Law

Though the Hebrews were obligated by the Law to tithe, God never intended tithing to become a mere act of duty performed apart from the heart. The tithe collected in the Israelite community, for example, actually went to support fellow Israelites.

> "For the tithe of the sons of Israel, which they offer as an offering to the Lord, I have given to the Levites for an inheritance; therefore I have said concerning them, 'They shall have no inheritance among the sons of Israel.'" (Num. 18:24)

The Levites had no inheritance of land among the Israelites. Their job was to care for the tabernacle; they didn't raise crops or livestock. So their sustenance had to come from the other Israelites. Hence the tithe. The Hebrews, then, not only showed their obedience to God by tithing, they provided for the Levites.

The Levites, in turn, were required to give one-tenth from their tithe to support the high priest (see vv. 26–29). In addition, every third year the tithe of the previous year was to be gathered and shared with the Levites and the destitute during a special festival (see Deut. 14:28–29).

By giving back a portion of the crops and livestock with which God had blessed them, the Israelites honored God as the provider of all their needs—and they took care of the needs of their community. You see? Tithing was a law, but it was a law with a heart and a purpose, at least until it was distorted by later Israelites.

> To these comparatively simple laws in the Pentateuch governing tithing there were added a host of minutiae which turned a beautiful religious principle into a grievous burden. . . . This unfortunate tendency in Israel undoubtedly contributed to the conviction that acceptance with God could be merited through such ritual observances as tithing (Lk. 11:42), without submitting to the moral law of justice, mercy and faith (Mt. 23:23f.).[1]

Tithing, however, wasn't the only provision for giving under the Mosaic Law. The Israelites were also encouraged to give for special occasions, such as the building of the tabernacle and freewill offerings—as their hearts moved them (see Exod. 25:1–9; 35:4–19; 36:4–7; Deut. 16:10; 2 Chron. 35:7–9).

God Took Tithing Seriously

Tithing was so important to God that He equated failure to do it with robbery.

> "Will a man rob God? Yet you are robbing Me! But you say, 'How have we robbed Thee?' In tithes and offerings." (Mal. 3:8)

The Israelites during Malachi's day had drifted from Him; they had stopped obeying His law, of which tithing was a part. In dismissing that part of the law, they were not only robbing God materially, they were robbing Him of His rightful place of prominence and reverence in the community.

---

1. J. G. S. S. Thomson, "Tithes," in *New Bible Dictionary*, 2d ed. (1982; reprint, Downers Grove, Ill.: InterVarsity Press, 1991), p. 1205.

A Similar Plan: The First-Century Church

Though Christ renounced the pharisaic method of tithing—which had become a heartless, legalistic obligation (see Matt. 23:23–24), He never rescinded tithing as a legitimate method of consistent giving (5:17). In fact, money was crucial for the survival and functioning of the early church. The New Testament clearly supports planned, systematic giving.

Systematic Giving

> Now concerning the collection for the saints, as I directed the churches of Galatia, so do you also. On the first day of every week let each one of you put aside and save, as he may prosper, that no collections be made when I come. And when I arrive, whomever you may approve, I shall send them with letters to carry your gift to Jerusalem; and if it is fitting for me to go also, they will go with me. (1 Cor. 16:1–4)

Paul isn't prescribing a percentage of gross income here. But he is supporting the deliberate, consistent setting aside of funds for the work of the ministry—in this case, helping the church at Jerusalem. Also, Paul's admonition to pay worthy elders "double honor" suggests a regular collection of funds to pay wages for their leaders' work in the church (see 1 Tim. 5:17–18).

Tithing is like any other good habit—we do it because we think it's important. And the best way to do it consistently is to work it into our family budget as well as make it a regular act of worship.

Spontaneous Offerings

Just as the Israelites supplemented their tithes with one-time gifts for special projects, so the early church supplemented their systematic giving with special offerings. Early believers, for example, shared their possessions with other members of the body, and sacrificial giving was the norm (see Acts 2:43–45; 4:36–37).

In today's church, whatever we put in the offering plate need not stifle us from responding to special needs as they come up. A little extra to a missionary family. A one-time donation to help paint the church building. A surge of congregational giving to get the church out of debt. Helping a family celebrate Christmas when they would otherwise have to go without gifts and a turkey dinner this year. A hot meal for a homeless person. Such special, spontaneous acts of giving can help remind us why we tithe in the first place.

 Living Insights

Right about now, those nagging, guilt-inducing voices may be starting to bounce around inside your head: "Man, what a slug I am; I'm not giving 10 percent. I can barely pay my bills." Or how about this one: "Good luck getting into heaven, buckaroo. You've slacked way off on your tithing." Or this one: "OK, if I sell the stereo, ditch the television set, and wear cheap suits, I'll be right with God again."

Don't listen to such accusations; they're from the Enemy. Listen instead to this voice:

> There is therefore now no condemnation for those who are in Christ Jesus. For the law of the Spirit of life in Christ Jesus has set you free from the law of sin and of death. (Rom. 8:1–2)

Our eternal security rests in the shed blood of Jesus Christ, not in our giving habits. So don't flagellate yourself if your giving practices fall below par. Instead, think of ways you might work toward giving more consistently and in proportion to your income.

Start by taking a look at your budget. Do you have one? Do you know where your money is going each month? You might be surprised at how generously and consistently you can give once you get a firm handle on your cash flow. If you don't know how to develop a budget, we've recommended some books in the bibliography that will help.

Do you see any expenses you can pare down to allow more room for giving? Could you go out to eat once a week instead of two or three times? Are you weighed down by heavy debt? How about formulating a plan to get out of it? Can you get a better deal on car or health or life insurance to create more discretionary income? Here's some space for writing and figuring.

_____

_____

_____

_____

_____

_____

_____

_____

_____

_____

Shaving expenses can provide more to give, but so can increasing your income. Is there anything you can do to generate some extra income—that is, without endangering your spiritual life or putting undue stress on yourself or family? Do you have a hobby—crafts, woodworking, creative writing—that you could parlay into some additional money? Or how about having a garage sale? It's amazing what people will pay for the junk we no longer want. What other opportunities do you see?

_____

_____

_____

_____

_____

_____

_____

_____

_____

Now, based on your financial situation, what's a realistic percentage for you to give each month? Five percent? Ten? More? Go ahead and enter the amount in your budget as a regular expense. You might want to start another category for saving just a little for the purpose of responding to special needs as they arise.

_____

_____

_____

_____

_____

Now you're all set to practice hilarious generosity. So smile. And give . . . as He has given to you.

BOOKS FOR
PROBING FURTHER

When you consider the vault-full of wisdom about money found in the Scriptures, we've only jingled a little bit of loose change. If you want to explore the topic more deeply, here are some resources to help you budget, save, spend, and give wisely.

Barnett, Jake. *Wealth and Wisdom: A Biblical Perspective on Possessions.* Colorado Springs, Colo.: NavPress, 1987.

Beisner, E. Calvin. *Prosperity and Poverty: The Compassionate Use of Resources in a World of Scarcity.* Westchester, Ill.: Crossway Books, 1988.

Blue, Ron. *Master Your Money: A Step-by-step Plan for Financial Freedom.* Nashville, Tenn.: Thomas Nelson Publishers, 1986.

———. *Taming the Money Monster: Five Steps to Conquering Debt.* Colorado Springs, Colo.: Focus on the Family Publishing, 1993.

Blue, Ron, and Judy Blue. *Money Matters for Parents and Their Kids.* Nashville, Tenn.: Thomas Nelson Publishers, Oliver Nelson, 1988.

———. *A Woman's Guide to Financial Peace of Mind.* Pomona, Calif.: Focus on the Family Publishing, 1991.

Burkett, Larry. *Answers to Your Family's Financial Questions.* Wheaton, Ill.: Tyndale House Publishers, Living Books, 1987.

———. *The Complete Financial Guide for Single Parents.* Wheaton, Ill.: Scripture Press Publications, Victor Books, 1991.

———. *The Complete Financial Guide for Young Couples.* Wheaton, Ill.: Scripture Press Publications, Victor Books, 1989.

———. *Debt-Free Living.* Chicago, Ill.: Moody Press, 1989.

Busby, Daniel D., Kent E. Barber, and Robert L. Temple. *The Christian's Guide to Worry-free Money Management.* Grand Rapids, Mich.: Zondervan Publishing House, 1994.

Campolo, Tony, and Gordon Aeschliman. *50 Ways You Can Feed a Hungry World.* Downers Grove, Ill.: InterVarsity Press, 1991.

Caywood, George. *Escaping Materialism: Living a Life That's Rich Toward God.* Sisters, Oreg.: Questar Publishers, 1989.

Getz, Gene A. *A Biblical Theology of Material Possessions.* Chicago, Ill.: Moody Press, 1990.

———. *Real Prosperity: Biblical Principles of Material Possessions.* Chicago, Ill.: Moody Press, 1990.

Kuyper, Abraham. *The Problem of Poverty.* Grand Rapids, Mich.: Baker Book House, 1991.

Neff, David, ed. *The Midas Trap.* Wheaton, Ill.: Scripture Press Publications, Victor Books, 1990.

Perkins, John M. *Beyond Charity: The Call to Christian Community Development.* Grand Rapids, Mich.: Baker Book House, Baker Books, 1993.

Ronsvalle, John, and Sylvia Ronsvalle. *Behind the Stained Glass Windows: Money Dynamics in the Church.* Grand Rapids, Mich.: Baker Book House, Baker Books, 1996.

———. *The Poor Have Faces: Loving Your Neighbor in the 21st Century.* Grand Rapids, Mich.: Baker Book House, 1992.

Schneider, John. *Godly Materialism: Rethinking Money and Possessions.* Downers Grove, Ill.: InterVarsity Press, 1994.

Tyson, Eric. *Personal Finance for Dummies.* Foster City, Calif.: IDG Books Worldwide, 1995.

Some of these books may be out of print and available only through a library. For those currently available, please contact your local Christian bookstore. Books by Charles R. Swindoll may be obtained through Insight for Living. IFL also offers some books by other authors—please note the ordering information that follows and contact the office that serves you.

ORDERING INFORMATION

HILARIOUS GENEROSITY
Cassette Tapes and Study Guide

This Bible study guide was designed to be used independently or in conjunction with the broadcast of Chuck Swindoll's taped messages which are listed below. If you would like to order cassette tapes or further copies of this study guide, please see the information given below and the order forms provided at the end of this guide.

		U.S.	Canada
HIG	Study guide	$ 4.95 ea.	$ 6.50 ea.
HIGCS	Cassette series, includes all individual tapes, album cover, and one complimentary study guide	16.00 ea.	20.46 ea.
HIG 1–2	Individual cassettes, includes messages A and B	6.00 ea.	7.48 ea.

Prices are subject to change without notice.

HIG   1-A: A Case for Joyful Generosity—Selected Scriptures
      B: Enjoying the Benefits of Generosity—
        1 Timothy 6:6–10, 17–19

HIG   2-A: Valuable Principles of Money Management—
        Selected Proverbs
      B: A Joyful Plan That Cannot Fail—Selected Scriptures

HOW TO ORDER BY PHONE OR FAX
(Credit card orders only)

Web site: http://www.insight.org

United States: 1-800-772-8888 or FAX (714) 575-5684, 24 hours a day, 7 days a week

Canada: 1-800-663-7639 or FAX (604) 532-7173, 24 hours a day, 7 days a week

Australia and the South Pacific: call (03) 9872-4606 from 8:00 A.M. to 5:00 P.M., Monday through Friday
FAX (03) 9874-8890, anytime, day or night

Other International Locations: call the International Ordering Services Department in the United States at (714) 575-5000 from 8:00 A.M. to 4:30 P.M., Pacific time, Monday through Friday
FAX (714) 575-5683 anytime, day or night

HOW TO ORDER BY MAIL

United States
• Mail to: Mail Center
Insight for Living
Post Office Box 69000
Anaheim, CA 92817-0900
• Sales tax: California residents add 7.75%.
• Shipping and handling charges must be added to each order. See chart on order form for amount.
• Payment: personal checks, money orders, credit cards (Visa, Master-Card, Discover Card, and American Express). No invoices or COD orders available.
• $10 fee for *any* returned check.

Canada
• Mail to: Insight for Living Ministries
Post Office Box 2510
Vancouver, BC V6B 3W7
• Sales tax: please add 7% GST. British Columbia residents also add 7% sales tax (on tapes or cassette series).
• Shipping and handling charges must be added to each order. See chart on order form for amount.
• Payment: personal cheques, money orders, credit cards (Visa, Master-Card). No invoices or COD orders available.
• Delivery: approximately four weeks.

Australia and the South Pacific
• Mail to: Insight for Living, Inc.
GPO Box 2823 EE
Melbourne, Victoria 3001, Australia
• Shipping: add 25% to the total order.
• Delivery: approximately four to six weeks.
• Payment: personal cheques payable in Australian funds, international money orders, or credit cards (Visa, MasterCard, and Bankcard).

United Kingdom and Europe
- Mail to: Insight for Living
  c/o Trans World Radio
  Post Office Box 1020
  Bristol, BS99 1XS
  England, United Kingdom
- Shipping: add 25% to the total order.
- Delivery: approximately four to six weeks.
- Payment: cheques payable in sterling pounds or credit cards (Visa, MasterCard, and American Express).

Other International Locations
- Mail to: International Processing Services Department
  Insight for Living
  Post Office Box 69000
  Anaheim, CA 92817-0900
- Shipping and delivery time: please see chart that follows.
- Payment: personal checks payable in U.S. funds, international money orders, or credit cards (Visa, MasterCard, and American Express).

Type of Shipping	Postage Cost	Delivery
Surface	10% of total order*	6 to 10 weeks
Airmail	25% of total order*	under 6 weeks

*Use U.S. price as a base.

Our Guarantee: Your complete satisfaction is our top priority here at Insight for Living. If you're not completely satisfied with anything you order, please return it for full credit, a refund, or a replacement, as you prefer.

Insight for Living Catalog: The Insight for Living catalog features study guides, tapes, and books by a variety of Christian authors. To obtain a free copy, call us at the numbers listed above.

Order Form
United States, Australia, and Other International Locations
(Canadian residents please use order form on reverse side.)

HIGCS represents the entire *Hilarious Generosity* series in a special album cover, while HIG 1–2 are the individual tapes included in the series. HIG represents this study guide, should you desire to order additional copies.

HIG	Study guide	$ 4.95 ea.
HIGCS	Cassette series, includes all individual tapes, album cover, and one complimentary study guide	16.00 ea.
HIG 1–2	Individual cassettes, includes messages A and B	6.00 ea.

Product Code	Product Description	Quantity	Unit Price	Total
			$	$

			Order Total	

Amount of Order	First Class	UPS	
$ 7.50 and under	1.00	4.00	UPS ❑ First Class ❑ *Shipping and handling must be added. See chart for charges.*
$ 7.51 to 12.50	1.50	4.25	**Subtotal**
$12.51 to 25.00	3.50	4.50	**California Residents—Sales Tax** *Add 7.75% of subtotal.*
$25.01 to 35.00	4.50	4.75	**Non-United States Residents** *Australia and Europe add 25%. All other locations: U.S. price plus 10% surface postage or 25% airmail.*
$35.01 to 60.00	5.50	5.25	
$60.01 to 99.99	6.50	5.75	
$100.00 and over	No charge		**Gift to Insight for Living** *Tax-deductible in the United States.*
			Total Amount Due *Please do not send cash.* $

Rush shipping and Fourth Class are also available. Please call for details.

Prices are subject to change without notice.

Payment by: ❑ Check or money order payable to Insight for Living   ❑ Credit card
(Circle one):   Visa   MasterCard   Discover Card   American Express   Bankcard (In Australia)

Number _____

Expiration Date _____   Signature _____
We cannot process your credit card purchase without your signature.

Name _____

Address _____

City _____   State _____

Zip Code _____   Country _____

Telephone (___) _____   Radio Station ____ ____ ____ ____
If questions arise concerning your order, we may need to contact you.

Mail this order form to the Mail Center at one of these addresses:

Insight for Living
Post Office Box 69000, Anaheim, CA 92817-0900

Insight for Living, Inc.
GPO Box 2823 EE, Melbourne, VIC 3001, Australia

ECFR MEMBER

Order Form
Canadian Residents

(Residents of the United States, Australia, and other international locations, please use order form on reverse side.)

HIGCS represents the entire *Hilarious Generosity* series in a special album cover, while HIG 1–2 are the individual tapes included in the series. HIG represents this study guide, should you desire to order additional copies.

HIG	Study guide	$ 6.50 ea.
HIGCS	Cassette series, includes all individual tapes, album cover, and one complimentary study guide	20.46 ea.
HIG 1–2	Individual cassettes, includes messages A and B	7.48 ea.

Product Code	Product Description	Quantity	Unit Price	Total
			$	$

Amount of Order	Canada Post		
Orders to $10.00	2.00	**Subtotal**	
$10.01 to 30.00	3.50	**Add 7% GST**	
$30.01 to 50.00	5.00	**British Columbia Residents** *Add 7% sales tax on individual tapes or cassette series.*	
$50.01 to 99.99	7.00	**Shipping** *Shipping and handling must be added. See chart for charges.*	
$100 and over	Free	**Gift to Insight for Living Ministries** *Tax-deductible in Canada.*	
		Total Amount Due *Please do not send cash.*	$

Loomis courier is also available. Please call for details.

Prices are subject to change without notice.

Payment by: ☐ Cheque or money order payable to Insight for Living Ministries
☐ Credit card

(Circle one): Visa   MasterCard   Number _____

Expiration Date _____   Signature _____
We cannot process your credit card purchase without your signature.

Name _____

Address _____

City _____   Province _____

Postal Code _____   Country _____

Telephone (____) _____   Radio Station ____ ____ ____ ____
If questions arise concerning your order, we may need to contact you.

Mail this order form to the Processing Services Department at the following address:

Insight for Living Ministries
Post Office Box 2510
Vancouver, BC, Canada V6B 3W7

Order Form
United States, Australia, and Other International Locations
(Canadian residents please use order form on reverse side.)

HIGCS represents the entire *Hilarious Generosity* series in a special album cover, while HIG 1–2 are the individual tapes included in the series. HIG represents this study guide, should you desire to order additional copies.

HIG	Study guide	$ 4.95 ea.
HIGCS	Cassette series, includes all individual tapes, album cover, and one complimentary study guide	16.00 ea.
HIG 1–2	Individual cassettes, includes messages A and B	6.00 ea.

Product Code	Product Description	Quantity	Unit Price	Total
			$	$

Amount of Order	First Class	UPS		Order Total	
			UPS ❏ First Class ❏ *Shipping and handling must be added. See chart for charges.*		
$ 7.50 and under	1.00	4.00			
$ 7.51 to 12.50	1.50	4.25	Subtotal		
$12.51 to 25.00	3.50	4.50	**California Residents—Sales Tax** *Add 7.75% of subtotal.*		
$25.01 to 35.00	4.50	4.75	**Non-United States Residents** *Australia and Europe add 25%. All other locations: U.S. price plus 10% surface postage or 25% airmail.*		
$35.01 to 60.00	5.50	5.25			
$60.01 to 99.99	6.50	5.75			
$100.00 and over	No charge		**Gift to Insight for Living** *Tax-deductible in the United States.*		
			Total Amount Due *Please do not send cash.*	$	

Rush shipping and Fourth Class are also available. Please call for details.

Prices are subject to change without notice.

Payment by: ❏ Check or money order payable to Insight for Living   ❏ Credit card
(Circle one):   Visa   MasterCard   Discover Card   American Express   Bankcard (In Australia)

Number _____

Expiration Date _____   Signature _____
We cannot process your credit card purchase without your signature.

Name _____

Address _____

City _____   State _____

Zip Code _____   Country _____

Telephone ( ) _____   Radio Station ____ ____ ____ ____
If questions arise concerning your order, we may need to contact you.

Mail this order form to the Mail Center at one of these addresses:

Insight for Living
Post Office Box 69000, Anaheim, CA 92817-0900

Insight for Living, Inc.
GPO Box 2823 EE, Melbourne, VIC 3001, Australia

ECFA MEMBER

Order Form
Canadian Residents

(Residents of the United States, Australia, and other international locations, please use order form on reverse side.)

HIGCS represents the entire *Hilarious Generosity* series in a special album cover, while HIG 1–2 are the individual tapes included in the series. HIG represents this study guide, should you desire to order additional copies.

HIG	Study guide	$ 6.50 ea.
HIGCS	Cassette series, includes all individual tapes, album cover, and one complimentary study guide	20.46 ea.
HIG 1–2	Individual cassettes, includes messages A and B	7.48 ea.

Product Code	Product Description	Quantity	Unit Price	Total
			$	$

Amount of Order	Canada Post		
		Subtotal	
		Add 7% GST	
Orders to $10.00	2.00	**British Columbia Residents** *Add 7% sales tax on individual tapes or cassette series.*	
$10.01 to 30.00	3.50		
$30.01 to 50.00	5.00	**Shipping** *Shipping and handling must be added. See chart for charges.*	
$50.01 to 99.99	7.00		
$100 and over	Free	**Gift to Insight for Living Ministries** *Tax-deductible in Canada.*	
		Total Amount Due *Please do not send cash.*	$

Loomis courier is also available. Please call for details.

Prices are subject to change without notice.

Payment by: ❑ Cheque or money order payable to Insight for Living Ministries
❑ Credit card

(Circle one): Visa   MasterCard   Number _____

Expiration Date _____   Signature _____
We cannot process your credit card purchase without your signature.

Name _____

Address _____

City _____   Province _____

Postal Code _____   Country _____

Telephone (____) _____   Radio Station ____ ____ ____ ____
If questions arise concerning your order, we may need to contact you.

Mail this order form to the Processing Services Department at the following address:

Insight for Living Ministries
Post Office Box 2510
Vancouver, BC, Canada V6B 3W7

Order Form
United States, Australia, and Other International Locations
(Canadian residents please use order form on reverse side.)

HIGCS represents the entire *Hilarious Generosity* series in a special album cover, while HIG 1–2 are the individual tapes included in the series. HIG represents this study guide, should you desire to order additional copies.

HIG	Study guide	$ 4.95 ea.
HIGCS	Cassette series, includes all individual tapes, album cover, and one complimentary study guide	16.00 ea.
HIG 1–2	Individual cassettes, includes messages A and B	6.00 ea.

Product Code	Product Description	Quantity	Unit Price	Total
			$	$

Amount of Order	First Class	UPS
$ 7.50 and under	1.00	4.00
$ 7.51 to 12.50	1.50	4.25
$12.51 to 25.00	3.50	4.50
$25.01 to 35.00	4.50	4.75
$35.01 to 60.00	5.50	5.25
$60.01 to 99.99	6.50	5.75
$100.00 and over	No charge	

Rush shipping and Fourth Class are also available. Please call for details.

Order Total	
UPS ❏ First Class ❏ *Shipping and handling must be added. See chart for charges.*	
Subtotal	
California Residents—Sales Tax *Add 7.75% of subtotal.*	
Non-United States Residents *Australia and Europe add 25%. All other locations: U.S. price plus 10% surface postage or 25% airmail.*	
Gift to Insight for Living *Tax-deductible in the United States.*	
Total Amount Due *Please do not send cash.*	$

Prices are subject to change without notice.

Payment by: ❏ Check or money order payable to Insight for Living   ❏ Credit card

(Circle one):   Visa   MasterCard   Discover Card   American Express   Bankcard (In Australia)

Number _____

Expiration Date _____   Signature _____
We cannot process your credit card purchase without your signature.

Name _____

Address _____

City _____   State _____

Zip Code _____   Country _____

Telephone (____) _____   Radio Station ____ ____ ____ ____
If questions arise concerning your order, we may need to contact you.

Mail this order form to the Mail Center at one of these addresses:

Insight for Living
Post Office Box 69000, Anaheim, CA 92817-0900

Insight for Living, Inc.
GPO Box 2823 EE, Melbourne, VIC 3001, Australia

ECFA

Order Form
Canadian Residents
(Residents of the United States, Australia, and other international locations,
please use order form on reverse side.)

HIGCS represents the entire *Hilarious Generosity* series in a special album cover, while HIG
1–2 are the individual tapes included in the series. HIG represents this study guide, should
you desire to order additional copies.

HIG	Study guide	$ 6.50 ea.
HIGCS	Cassette series,	20.46 ea.
	includes all individual tapes, album cover,	
	and one complimentary study guide	
HIG 1–2	Individual cassettes,	7.48 ea.
	includes messages A and B	

Product Code	Product Description	Quantity	Unit Price	Total
			$	$

Amount of Order	Canada Post		
Orders to $10.00	2.00	**Subtotal**	
		Add 7% GST	
$10.01 to 30.00	3.50	**British Columbia Residents** *Add 7% sales tax on individual tapes or cassette series.*	
$30.01 to 50.00	5.00		
$50.01 to 99.99	7.00	**Shipping** *Shipping and handling must be added. See chart for charges.*	
$100 and over	Free		
		Gift to Insight for Living Ministries *Tax-deductible in Canada.*	
		Total Amount Due *Please do not send cash.*	$

Loomis courier is also available.
Please call for details.

Prices are subject to change without notice.

Payment by: ☐ Cheque or money order payable to Insight for Living Ministries
☐ Credit card

(Circle one): Visa   MasterCard   Number _____

Expiration Date _____   Signature _____
We cannot process your credit card purchase without your signature.

Name _____

Address _____

City _____   Province _____

Postal Code _____   Country _____

Telephone (____) _____   Radio Station ____ ____ ____ ____
If questions arise concerning your order, we may need to contact you.

Mail this order form to the Processing Services Department at the following address:

Insight for Living Ministries
Post Office Box 2510
Vancouver, BC, Canada V6B 3W7